THANKS BE TO GOD

THANKS BE TO GOD:
A THIRTY DAY JOURNAL

J.M. MCCLOGHRY

thanks

/THaNGks/

noun

plural noun: thanks

1. an expression of gratitude

It's clear throughout the Bible that thankfulness is part of the Christian life. We find it mentioned over 70 times in the New Testament, 20 times in the gospels alone, and we learn through these scriptures that thankfulness is for every season. So then the question for the believer becomes: how do I make thankfulness a part of my everyday life? How does it become so ingrained in my language and heart that it not only changes me but it flows out of me and immerses the people around me? I would suggest to you that forming the habit of thankfulness will change the way you live and view the life God has given you to walk through. Studies have shown that repetition, or practice, solidifies new habits into our lives. In fact, they show that forming good (and bad) habits depends more on how often you perform an action than on how much satisfaction you get from it. I believe as you and I form the habit of beginning with "Thanks be to God" every day it will change us from the inside out, forming a habit of intentional thankfulness in every season. You're invited to journey through these 30 days and see how God changes your life through His living word.

J.M. McCloghry

ONE

GRATITUDE

"Remember this: Whoever sows sparingly will also reap sparingly, and whoever sows generously will also reap generously. Each of you should give what you have decided in your heart to give, not reluctantly or under compulsion, for God loves a cheerful giver. And God is able to bless you abundantly, so that in all things at all times, having all that you need, you will abound in every good work. As it is written: "They have freely scattered their gifts to the poor; their righteousness endures forever.""

2 CORINTHIANS 9:6-9 NIV

Thanks be to God for seed to sow. Thank you, God, that you fill my life with everything I need today. I also thank you for not giving me everything that I want, but only what I need. Help me to live my life generously as a reflection of a heart that knows my God is able to bless me abundantly. Thank you that this blessing equips me to abound in every good work that you lead me to put my hands to.

THANKS
BE TO
GOD

TWO

GENEROSITY

"Now he who supplies seed to the sower and bread for food will also supply and increase your store of seed and will enlarge the harvest of your righteousness. You will be enriched in every way so that you can be generous on every occasion, and through us your generosity will result in thanksgiving to God. This service that you perform is not only supplying the needs of the Lord's people but is also overflowing in many expressions of thanks to God. Because of the service by which you have proved yourselves, others will praise God for the obedience that accompanies your confession of the gospel of Christ, and for your generosity in sharing with them and with everyone else. And in their prayers for you their hearts will go out to you, because of the surpassing grace God has given you. Thanks be to God for his indescribable gift!"

2 CORINTHIANS 9:10-15 NIV

Thanks be to God for a generosity that produces more seed to be generous with, increasing a harvest of righteousness through Jesus, in my life. Thank you, God, that my generosity results in thanksgiving. I am thankful today that my generosity becomes and expression of thanks to my Holy God. Thanks be to God for this indescribable gift that allows me to be a part of the story of your grace and love for the world.

THANKS
BE TO
GOD

THREE

THANKS

"I declare to you, brothers and sisters, that flesh and blood cannot inherit the kingdom of God, nor does the perishable inherit the imperishable. Listen, I tell you a mystery: We will not all sleep, but we will all be changed— in a flash, in the twinkling of an eye, at the last trumpet. For the trumpet will sound, the dead will be raised imperishable, and we will be changed. For the perishable must clothe itself with the imperishable, and the mortal with immortality. When the perishable has been clothed with the imperishable, and the mortal with immortality, then the saying that is written will come true: "Death has been swallowed up in victory." "Where, O death, is your victory? Where, O death, is your sting?" The sting of death is sin, and the power of sin is the law. But thanks be to God! He gives us the victory through our Lord Jesus Christ. Therefore, my dear brothers and sisters, stand firm. Let nothing move you. Always give yourselves fully to the work of the Lord, because you know that your labor in the Lord is not in vain."

1 CORINTHIANS 15:50-58 NIV

Thanks be to God for an eternal kingdom, eternal life, and death that has been swallowed up in victory. Thanks be to God who has given me victory today though His Son, Jesus. God, I declare with thanks, your victory over the battles in my life. Thank you, God, for giving me the strength to stand firm. I labor the work of this gospel of grace today, knowing that it is not in vain. Thank you, God, for equipping me to labor with the rhythms of grace, until my last breath.

THANKS
BE TO
GOD

FOUR

THANKSGIVING AND COMMUNITY

"Thanks be to God, who put into the heart of Titus the same concern I have for you. For Titus not only welcomed our appeal, but he is coming to you with much enthusiasm and on his own initiative. And we are sending along with him the brother who is praised by all the churches for his service to the gospel. What is more, he was chosen by the churches to accompany us as we carry the offering, which we administer in order to honor the Lord himself and to show our eagerness to help. We want to avoid any criticism of the way we administer this liberal gift. For we are taking pains to do what is right, not only in the eyes of the Lord but also in the eyes of man."

2 CORINTHIANS 8:16-21 NIV

Thanks be to God for Godly accountability through the saints. Thank you, God, that you have put people in my world to love me enthusiastically, with excellence even when there are hard things to hear. Thank you, God, that you have chosen people to be in my world that are willing to take pains to deliver messages to me and do right in the eyes of the Lord and man. Help me to hear hard things with a soft heart and and receive Godly correction and instruction with grace and a heart to change. Thank you, God, that you are making me more like you and using others to be a part of that process. Thank you, God, that life is a process.

THANKS
BE TO
GOD

FIVE

KNOWLEDGE

"But thanks be to God, who always leads us as captives in Christ's triumphal procession and uses us to spread the aroma of the knowledge of him everywhere. For we are to God the pleasing aroma of Christ among those who are being saved and those who are perishing. To the one we are an aroma that brings death; to the other, an aroma that brings life. And who is equal to such a task? Unlike so many, we do not peddle the word of God for profit. On the contrary, in Christ we speak before God with sincerity, as those sent from God."

2 CORINTHIANS 2:14-17 NIV

Thanks be to God that we are the pleasing aroma of Christ. Thank you, Lord, that you have made us to know you and love you. You have created us to carry your likeness and spread the aroma of our knowledge of you everywhere. Help me to grow in knowledge of you so that I can do this everywhere I go. God, I choose to speak with all sincerity because I know I was made by you and sent to be a light to my world, by you.

THANKS
BE TO
GOD

SIX

FREEDOM FROM SIN

"What then? Shall we sin because we are not under the law but under grace? By no means! Don't you know that when you offer yourselves to someone as obedient slaves, you are slaves of the one you obey—whether you are slaves to sin, which leads to death, or to obedience, which leads to righteousness? But thanks be to God that, though you used to be slaves to sin, you have come to obey from your heart the pattern of teaching that has now claimed your allegiance. You have been set free from sin and have become slaves to righteousness."

ROMANS 6:15-18 NIV

Thanks be to God that I am no longer a slave to sin. I was trapped in sin and darkness, my sin was taking me straight to death - but you saved me. I declare today, you have my complete allegiance. I am no longer a slave to sin, but now to righteousness. Thank you, Jesus, that I have been made right by you. My heart sees the pattern of your teaching and from my heart I live a life of obedience to you.

THANKS
BE TO
GOD

SEVEN

SURRENDER

"So I find this law at work: Although I want to do good, evil is right there with me. For in my inner being I delight in God's law; but I see another law at work in me, waging war against the law of my mind and making me a prisoner of the law of sin at work within me. What a wretched man I am! Who will rescue me from this body that is subject to death? Thanks be to God, who delivers me through Jesus Christ our Lord! So then, I myself in my mind am a slave to God's law, but in my sinful nature a slave to the law of sin."

ROMANS 7:21-25 NIV

Thanks be to God that though I cannot in my own strength, you can. Where I am unable, you are always able. Though my body fail, my God does not. Where my will fails, God will never fail. Thanks be to God that this body would have held me prisoner to what I did not desire, but I was rescued, delivered and freed by Jesus Christ my Lord! I give my will to you today, my God. I give my thanks that though I cannot, you can. I live not through my own strength, but through yours.

THANKS
BE TO
GOD

EIGHT

THANKS TO THE GOD OF ALL

"Give thanks to the Lord, for he is good. His love endures forever. Give thanks to the God of gods. His love endures forever. Give thanks to the Lord of Lords: His love endures forever. to him who alone does great wonders, His love endures forever. who by his understanding made the heavens, His love endures forever. who spread out the earth upon the waters, His love endures forever. who made the great lights— His love endures forever. the sun to govern the day, His love endures forever. the moon and stars to govern the night; His love endures forever."

ROMANS 7:21-25 NIV

Thanks be to God, the God of enduring love. Your love is everlasting. When I look at the heavens, the wonderful and wondrous things you have made, I cannot fathom what you have done. I cannot understand how such wonders are created by your word. I am in awe of you, God. Your love for me is a gift from the One who created everything I see. Who am I that you would love me so and still you do. You made the sun to govern the day and the moon and stars to govern the night. Thank you God that these wonders remind me of your love that goes on and on through the day and the night. I give thanks to you and for your love that endures forever.

THANKS
BE TO
GOD

NINE

LIVING IN THANKS

"Be very careful, then, how you live—not as unwise but as wise, making the most of every opportunity, because the days are evil. Therefore do not be foolish, but understand what the Lord's will is. Do not get drunk on wine, which leads to debauchery. Instead, be filled with the Spirit, speaking to one another with psalms, hymns, and songs from the Spirit. Sing and make music from your heart to the Lord, always giving thanks to God the Father for everything, in the name of our Lord Jesus Christ."

EPHESIANS 5:15-20 NIV

Thanks be to God, for you show me how to live. I want to live in wisdom. When I need wisdom, you are the one I run to. You are the giver of wisdom. God, help me to understand what your will is for my life. I choose, as a lover of wisdom, to obey you. I choose not to fill my body or mind with anything that would lead to unwise decisions. I fill my life with what draws me closer to you, makes me want to tell others about you, and makes me a light where I am for your glory and purpose. I remember today that I was made by you and for you. To know you and to make you known. I don't want to be filled with any other spirit than the Holy Spirit. I want songs and thanks to flow from my whole life as I am fully immersed in you, God. Your wisdom and goodness leads me to a life built on a foundation that will not be shaken no matter what comes my way. When life is hard, I fill my heart with you. I choose not to numb away or drown the pain but to deliver it to your feet and watch your love, mercy, kindness, grace and healing hands at work. Thanks be to God who shows me how to live.

THANKS
BE TO
GOD

TEN

THANKS WITH LITTLE AND WITH MUCH

"I am not saying this because I am in need, for I have learned to be content whatever the circumstances. I know what it is to be in need, and I know what it is to have plenty. I have learned the secret of being content in any and every situation, whether well fed or hungry, whether living in plenty or in want. I can do all this through him who gives me strength."

PHILIPPIANS 4:11-13 NIV

Thanks be to God for provision in every season. You are God my provider, God who knows exactly what I need. Thank you, God, that there is not one area of my life that you haven't prepared me for and prepared the provision for me. I don't need to worry because you are a good Father. Even in seasons where I'm waiting to see how you will move, I know that you will move. So I wait in confidence and I wait in peace. I remind myself of how you've come through in my past as I watch for how you will show up in my future. I can do everything through You, my God, who gives me strength.

THANKS
BE TO
GOD

ELEVEN

THANKS IN THE MIDDLE OF THE STORM

"On the fourteenth night we were still being driven across the Adriatic Sea, when about midnight the sailors sensed they were approaching land. They took soundings and found that the water was a hundred and twenty feet deep. A short time later they took soundings again and found it was ninety feet deep. Fearing that we would be dashed against the rocks, they dropped four anchors from the stern and prayed for daylight. In an attempt to escape from the ship, the sailors let the lifeboat down into the sea, pretending they were going to lower some anchors from the bow. Then Paul said to the centurion and the soldiers, "Unless these men stay with the ship, you cannot be saved." So the soldiers cut the ropes that held the lifeboat and let it drift away. Just before dawn Paul urged them all to eat. "For the last fourteen days," he said, "you have been in constant suspense and have gone without food—you haven't eaten anything. Now I urge you to take some food. You need it to survive. Not one of you will lose a single hair from his head." After he said this, he took some bread and gave thanks to God in front of them all. Then he broke it and began to eat. They were all encouraged and ate some food themselves. Altogether there were 276 of us on board. When they had eaten as much as they wanted, they lightened the ship by throwing the grain into the sea."

ACTS 27:27-38 NIV

Thanks be to God in the middle of the storm. When I face the uncertainty of the storms that rage in my life, I have certainty in you God who will never leave or forsake me. Thanks be to God that you provide what I need and the wisdom and instruction through your word and Godly people you put in my life to know what to do and when to do it. Even in the middle of tension, you show me the provision you have for me and I can rise up in the middle of adversity and give thanks to you, God. Thanks be to my God who is in the middle of the storm with me.

THANKS
BE TO
GOD

TWELVE

SAVED TO GIVE THANKS

"Save us, Lord our God, and gather us from the nations, that we may give thanks to your holy name and glory in your praise. Praise be to the Lord, the God of Israel, from everlasting to everlasting. Let all the people say, "Amen!" Praise the Lord."
PSALMS 106:47-48 NIV

Thanks be to God for my salvation. All over the world, every nation, tribe and tongue will know your salvation, Lord. I look for the day that you gather your people from all across the earth to give thanks to your holy name and glory in your praise. Today, I choose to praise you and to thank you, God of Israel, that you are from everlasting to everlasting. Your love and mercy endures forever. You are the alpha and the omega, the beginning and the end.

THANKS
BE TO
GOD

THIRTEEN

THANKS FOR THE PROMISED JESUS

"The child's father and mother marveled at what was said about him. Then Simeon blessed them and said to Mary, his mother: "This child is destined to cause the falling and rising of many in Israel, and to be a sign that will be spoken against, so that the thoughts of many hearts will be revealed. And a sword will pierce your own soul too." There was also a prophet, Anna, the daughter of Penuel, of the tribe of Asher. She was very old; she had lived with her husband seven years after her marriage, and then was a widow until she was eighty-four. She never left the temple but worshiped night and day, fasting and praying. Coming up to them at that very moment, she gave thanks to God and spoke about the child to all who were looking forward to the redemption of Jerusalem."

LUKE 2:33-38 NIV

Thanks be to God who sent His only son, Jesus. Thanks be to God who invited His people to be a part of the story. God, may I be on the side of the story that worships and expects you. Let me be found in your house praying and fasting, longing for the redeemers story to invade the world around us. Thanks be to God that we pray and you hear us. We thank you that you have already sent and are sending our salvation.

THANKS
BE TO
GOD

FOURTEEN

THANKS BE TO GOD FOR JESUS WHO IS COMING TO REIGN

"The seventh angel sounded his trumpet, and there were loud voices in heaven, which said: "The kingdom of the world has become the kingdom of our Lord and of his Messiah, and he will reign for ever and ever." And the twenty-four elders, who were seated on their thrones before God, fell on their faces and worshiped God, saying: "We give thanks to you, Lord God Almighty, the One who is and who was, because you have taken your great power and have begun to reign."

REVELATION 11:15-17 NIV

Thanks be to God for my king who is coming to reign. I give thanks to you, Lord God Almighty, the one who is and who was. You reign over me and I pray for the day that you come back again. Come quickly, Lord. We long for the day that you come shining like the sun, riding on the white horse. We long for the day of no more weeping or pain. Until that day, God, I thank you that you are with me and you have called me to both know you and make you known to the world around me. I pray that I would be the kind of Christian that is passionate about everyone knowing the good news of the gospel of Jesus Christ, that none would perish but have everlasting life.

THANKS
BE TO
GOD

FIFTEEN

THANKS BE TO GOD FOR THE WORD OF GOD DWELLING RICHLY AMONG US

"Let the peace of Christ rule in your hearts, since as members of one body you were called to peace. And be thankful. Let the message of Christ dwell among you richly as you teach and admonish one another with all wisdom through psalms, hymns, and songs from the Spirit, singing to God with gratitude in your hearts. And whatever you do, whether in word or deed, do it all in the name of the Lord Jesus, giving thanks to God the Father through him."

COLOSSIANS 3:15-17 NIV

Thanks be to God the Father, through Jesus Christ the Son. I am thankful today for peace that comes from Christ. Where you are, even in the storm, there is peace because you are the Prince of Peace. Likewise, being made in your image, I am called to peace and thankfulness. I am called to a life richly dwelling with Jesus. When you call us to admonish one another, I pray that my life would be full of hearing from your word and from believers you have put in my world - correction and redirection in the way you call me. I don't want to live with blind spots because growth is hard. I don't want to do this alone or become offended when you send Godly correction, admonishment, to get me back on track. Help me to hear it through your church, through teaching, through song. I choose to sing through the highs and lows - singing to God a with grateful heart. Let all that I do in my words and actions be done in the name of Jesus, as I continue a life of thanks to Him.

THANKS
BE TO
GOD

SIXTEEN

SHOUTS OF PRAISE

"Let the heavens rejoice, let the earth be glad; let them say among the nations, "The Lord reigns!" Let the sea resound, and all that is in it; let the fields be jubilant, and everything in them! Let the trees of the forest sing, let them sing for joy before the Lord, for he comes to judge the earth. Give thanks to the Lord, for he is good; his love endures forever. Cry out, "Save us, God our Savior; gather us and deliver us from the nations, that we may give thanks to your holy name, and glory in your praise." Praise be to the Lord, the God of Israel, from everlasting to everlasting. Then all the people said "Amen" and "Praise the Lord.""

COLOSSIANS 3:15-17 NIV

Thanks be to God for your love endures forever. Your love began before I took my first breath and it will continue into eternity. It didn't begin at my life, it was prepared for me before I ever existed here on earth. The heavens rejoice, the earth is glad, the sea resounds and everything in it, the fields are full of joy because of your great love. The whole earth and everything in it gives thanks for your love endures forever. I give thanks to you God, I cry out thanks and praise for you have delivered us through your son Jesus and I praise His holy name. You are always and forever, everlasting to everlasting and I say AMEN - so be it - and I praise you, Lord.

THANKS
BE TO
GOD

SEVENTEEN

THANKSGIVING AND PRAYER

"I thank my God every time I remember you. In all my prayers for all of you, I always pray with joy because of your partnership in the gospel from the first day until now, being confident of this, that he who began a good work in you will carry it on to completion until the day of Christ Jesus. It is right for me to feel this way about all of you, since I have you in my heart and, whether I am in chains or defending and confirming the gospel, all of you share in God's grace with me. God can testify how I long for all of you with the affection of Christ Jesus. And this is my prayer: that your love may abound more and more in knowledge and depth of insight, so that you may be able to discern what is best and may be pure and blameless for the day of Christ, filled with the fruit of righteousness that comes through Jesus Christ—to the glory and praise of God."

LUKE 2:33-38 NIV

Thanks be to God for the shared work of the gospel. Thank you God for community, friends, and co-laborers to remember with thanks. I pray for joy as I partner with people from around the corner to around the world and watch you do what only you can do. I pray for the weary and the worn out to be strengthened by your strength. I pray for those doing the work of the ministry to continue in joy and find gratitude knowing we are all in this together. I give thanks in my heart in hard times and good times because we share in God's grace together and I pray that our love for the Lord and each other would only continue to grow. God, I pray that we would be filled to overflowing with the fruit that comes from being cultivated in your garden and it would all be to the praise of our God.

THANKS
BE TO
GOD

EIGHTEEN

A SACRIFICE OF THANKS

"Sacrifice thank offerings to God, fulfill your vows to the Most High, and call on me in the day of trouble; I will deliver you, and you will honor me."

LUKE 2:33-38 NIV

Thanks be to God for His response to my offerings. Thank you, God, that you invite me to lay down my life before you. I give you thanks that you do not force us to be yours, but you invite us. I give thanks that you don't stand far off needing nothing from us but that you delight in our offerings. I pray that you would show me how to give you that kind of offering that is true and worthy - that costs me something. I pray that my offerings of thanks would not just be when it is easy to find a reason to give thanks but also when it is hard to see my thankfulness for the trouble around me. You teach me through offering praise in pain, and thanks in trouble, that even in the struggle and storm you surround me. I will give thanks to you, I will call on you. You will deliver me and I will honor you always.

THANKS
BE TO
GOD

NINETEEN

THANKS FOR THE FAITH OF THE SAINTS

"We always thank God, the Father of our Lord Jesus Christ, when we pray for you, because we have heard of your faith in Christ Jesus and of the love you have for all God's people— the faith and love that spring from the hope stored up for you in heaven and about which you have already heard in the true message of the gospel that has come to you. In the same way, the gospel is bearing fruit and growing throughout the whole world—just as it has been doing among you since the day you heard it and truly understood God's grace."
COLOSSIANS 1:3-6 NIV

Thanks be to God for the faith in Christ Jesus I see in the people of God around me. For the gospel that grows in each one of them. I pray today for the believers in Christ and for their faith to grow. I pray my own faith would be strengthened as well. This gospel is a seed sown in the good soil of the heart of every believer. This gospel doesn't wither or die, but grows and is growing even now as I pray. This gospel of grace is bearing fruit and growing around the world and we are all connected and a part of it. Thank you, God, that we get to be a part of the Gospel going forth and bringing hope and salvation to the world.

THANKS
BE TO
GOD

TWENTY

THANKS FOR THE MIRACLE OF GOD HEARING US

"Jesus, once more deeply moved, came to the tomb. It was a cave with a stone laid across the entrance. "Take away the stone," he said. "But, Lord," said Martha, the sister of the dead man, "by this time there is a bad odor, for he has been there four days." Then Jesus said, "Did I not tell you that if you believe, you will see the glory of God?" So they took away the stone. Then Jesus looked up and said, "Father, I thank you that you have heard me. I knew that you always hear me, but I said this for the benefit of the people standing here, that they may believe that you sent me." When he had said this, Jesus called in a loud voice, "Lazarus, come out!" The dead man came out, his hands and feet wrapped with strips of linen, and a cloth around his face. Jesus said to them, "Take off the grave clothes and let him go.""

JOHN 11:38-44 NIV

Thanks be to God that you hear us. Even though you could remain far off, even though you are so high and exalted, holy and righteous, you choose to be God who is a Father to your children. You love to come close and to draw me near to yourself. When I weep, you are God who is right there weeping with me. You know my pain and even sent your Son to this earth to put on flesh and dwell with us. He suffered and died and took on pain and hurt to become the salvation of the earth to the glory of the Father. I am so thankful that you are my God. You hear and you redeem even that which seems lost. Help me to trust you both when I see the miracles I call out for answered this side of heaven or when I step into heaven and home. I know, my God, that you hear and you always answer and I trust how you answer me today.

THANKS
BE TO
GOD

TWENTY-ONE

THANKS BE TO GOD FOR CALLING US

"I thank Christ Jesus our Lord, who has given me strength, that he considered me trustworthy, appointing me to his service. Even though I was once a blasphemer and a persecutor and a violent man, I was shown mercy because I acted in ignorance and unbelief. The grace of our Lord was poured out on me abundantly, along with the faith and love that are in Christ Jesus. Here is a trustworthy saying that deserves full acceptance: Christ Jesus came into the world to save sinners— of whom I am the worst. But for that very reason I was shown mercy so that in me, the worst of sinners, Christ Jesus might display his immense patience as an example for those who would believe in him and receive eternal life. Now to the King eternal, immortal, invisible, the only God, be honor and glory for ever and ever. Amen."

1 TIMOTHY 1:12-17 NIV

Thanks be to God who gives me strength to be who He has called me to be. To Him who makes me able to be called strong, trustworthy, and appoints me to His service. I am thankful today that my past does not determine my future and that it has no hold over me that the power of Jesus isn't able to break. Nothing is too strong for my God. Thanks be to God that Jesus came into the world to save me and found me in His mercy. I pray that my life would be a display of your patience to love and save a sinner like me and show all those around me the goodness of who you are.

THANKS
BE TO
GOD

TWENTY TWO

THANKS BE TO GOD WHO HAS MADE US LEVITES TO PRAISE MORNING AND EVENING

"The duty of the Levites was to help Aaron's descendants in the service of the temple of the Lord: to be in charge of the courtyards, the side rooms, the purification of all sacred things and the performance of other duties at the house of God. They were in charge of the bread set out on the table, the special flour for the grain offerings, the thin loaves made without yeast, the baking and the mixing, and all measurements of quantity and size. They were also to stand every morning to thank and praise the Lord. They were to do the same in the evening and whenever burnt offerings were presented to the Lord on the Sabbaths, at the New Moon feasts and at the appointed festivals. They were to serve before the Lord regularly in the proper number and in the way prescribed for them. And so the Levites carried out their responsibilities for the tent of meeting, for the Holy Place and, under their relatives the descendants of Aaron, for the service of the temple of the Lord."

1 CHRONICLES 23:28-32 NIV

Thanks be to God who has made me to praise Him. I was made to be a worshipper. I am a called to serve the Lord through my worship. It is not just my Sunday, but it is my whole life. Show me God how to serve you in your house for your glory and your pleasure. Show me how you love to be worshipped - in Spirit and truth, with all my heart, soul, mind, and strength. I am a Levite who is made to worship you and lead the worship of God in my home and world, morning to evening. Thank you, God, for showing me how you love to be worshipped and for hearing our praise.

THANKS
BE TO
GOD

TWENTY-THREE

THANKING GOD FOR THE GENERATIONAL LEGACY THAT I LIVE IN

"I thank God, whom I serve, as my ancestors did, with a clear conscience, as night and day I constantly remember you in my prayers. Recalling your tears, I long to see you, so that I may be filled with joy. I am reminded of your sincere faith, which first lived in your grandmother Lois and in your mother Eunice and, I am persuaded, now lives in you also."

2 TIMOTHY 1:3-5 NIV

Thanks be to God for generations upon generations of people who have served God. Thank you God that whether or not there are generations of believers in my family by blood or by faith, I am a part of something bigger than just myself. Thank you, God, that I look back on heroes of the faith who have sincerely lived for you and am encouraged and strengthened to keep going and not give up. Thank you for a history that tells the story of your faithfulness and provision for your people. Thank you that you are still the same God that provided for your people then and that does now. Praise God that I am a part of a story that is still being written and I thank you that you are the author of every part of my story.

THANKS
BE TO
GOD

TWENTY-FOUR

THANKS BE TO GOD FOR HUMILITY

"To some who were confident of their own righteousness and looked down on everyone else, Jesus told this parable: "Two men went up to the temple to pray, one a Pharisee and the other a tax collector. The Pharisee stood by himself and prayed: 'God, I thank you that I am not like other people—robbers, evildoers, adulterers—or even like this tax collector. I fast twice a week and give a tenth of all I get.' "But the tax collector stood at a distance. He would not even look up to heaven, but beat his breast and said, 'God, have mercy on me, a sinner.' "I tell you that this man, rather than the other, went home justified before God. For all those who exalt themselves will be humbled, and those who humble themselves will be exalted.""

LUKE 18:9-14 NIV

Thanks be to God that shows us what humility looks like, who honors humility over arrogance. It is not the parading and shouting like a pious Pharisee, lifting ourselves up above another. It is the humility to come before God and understand it is His mercy and salvation through His son Jesus that justifies us. I pray humility would be a marker of my relationship with you, God, and I would only ever be lifted up by lifting you up.

THANKS
BE TO
GOD

TWENTY-FIVE

THANKS BE TO GOD THAT HE CAUSES OUR FAITH TO GROW

"We ought always to thank God for you, brothers and sisters, and rightly so, because your faith is growing more and more, and the love all of you have for one another is increasing. Therefore, among God's churches we boast about your perseverance and faith in all the persecutions and trials you are enduring."

2 Thessalonians 1:3-4 NIV

Thanks be to God for the community God has placed me in. I look around and I see you in it, God. I see you in the loneliness that is broken with the sound of a message or call from a friend. I see you in the way we care and are cared for by others. Thank you, God, for the days when I need a friend and you send them. And thank you for the times when I am the friend that is sent. God, you give me the courage to be vulnerable and let people in even when it's hard. You help me to see the people that you put around me right now and to keep having the eyes to see that I'm not alone when the persecution and trials come. Thank you, God, that I'm not alone. And I don't have to believe the lie that I'm alone in this life. You love community and you love your church. Thank you for the brothers and sisters there that are so much more than a community: they are a family.

THANKS
BE TO
GOD

TWENTY-SIX

THANKS BE TO GOD THAT WE ARE ABLE TO RECEIVE THE WORD OF GOD

"And we also thank God continually because, when you received the word of God, which you heard from us, you accepted it not as a human word, but as it actually is, the word of God, which is indeed at work in you who believe."
1 Thessalonians 2:13 NIV

Thanks be to God that we receive the word of God. I love your word.

Just like the Psalms say, "Oh how I love your law! It is my meditation all the day. Your commandment makes me wiser than my enemies, for it is ever with me. I have more understanding than all my teachers, for your testimonies are my meditation. I understand more than the aged, for I keep your precepts. I hold back my feet from every evil way, in order to keep your word. I do not turn aside from your rules, for you have taught me. How sweet are your words to my taste, sweeter than honey to my mouth! Through your precepts I get understanding; therefore I hate every false way."
Psalm 119:97-104 ESV

I love your word, God, and I love receiving it into my heart. I love that you are at work through your word and in my life.

THANKS
BE TO
GOD

TWENTY-SEVEN

THANKS BE TO GOD THAT HE RESTORES TO THE DESOLATE, LAND THROUGH JESUS CHRIST

"This is what the Lord says: 'You say about this place, "It is a desolate waste, without people or animals." Yet in the towns of Judah and the streets of Jerusalem that are deserted, inhabited by neither people nor animals, there will be heard once more the sounds of joy and gladness, the voices of bride and bridegroom, and the voices of those who bring thank offerings to the house of the Lord, saying, "Give thanks to the Lord Almighty, for the Lord is good; his love endures forever." For I will restore the fortunes of the land as they were before,' says the Lord. "This is what the Lord Almighty says: 'In this place, desolate and without people or animals—in all its towns there will again be pastures for shepherds to rest their flocks. In the towns of the hill country, of the western foothills and of the Negev, in the territory of Benjamin, in the villages around Jerusalem and in the towns of Judah, flocks will again pass under the hand of the one who counts them,' says the Lord. " 'The days are coming,' declares the Lord, 'when I will fulfill the good promise I made to the people of Israel and Judah. " 'In those days and at that time I will make a righteous Branch sprout from David's line; he will do what is just and right in the land. In those days Judah will be saved and Jerusalem will live in safety. This is the name by which it will be called: The Lord Our Righteous Savior.'""

JEREMIAH 33:10-16 NIV

Thanks be to God for Jesus, my restorer and redeemer. Thank you, God, that I am alive today as one who has heard the story of Jesus who came and is our restorer. Jesus, who is the righteous branch to sprout from David's vine, who does what is right and just, who gives me safety. I call you today: my Lord and righteous Savior. Jesus, you came and you are coming back again. Everything I wait for to be made right when you come again is what I hope for. Thank you, Lord, that you saved me and rescued me from sin and death and that I am here to tell the story of your love and mercy. Thank you, Lord, that I know one day there will be no more suffering. Until that day, I will go into all the world and share the gospel, that none should perish but all have everlasting life in you. As C.T. Studd said, "Some want to live within the sound of church or chapel bell; I want to run a rescue shop, within a yard of hell." Lord, find me telling the world that you are the restorer and redeemer and you came for us all.

TWENTY-EIGHT

THANKS BE TO GOD FOR THE BOUNDARIES THAT PROTECT AND DIRECT MY LIFE

"You are my portion, Lord; I have promised to obey your words. I have sought your face with all my heart; be gracious to me according to your promise. I have considered my ways and have turned my steps to your statutes. I will hasten and not delay to obey your commands. Though the wicked bind me with ropes, I will not forget your law. At midnight I rise to give you thanks for your righteous laws. I am a friend to all who fear you, to all who follow your precepts. The earth is filled with your love, Lord; teach me your decrees."

PSALMS 119:57-64 NIV

Thanks be to God for my God who shows me through His word how to live this life. Thanks be to God for obedience that comes with a promise. God, you are enough for me. When my heart is wandering and I seek you, I know that I find you gracious towards me. Not because I deserve it over and over, but because it is who you are. Help me be quick to obey your commands, even when it feels like I'm pinned into a corner. Help me to embrace a holy fear of you and to follow your instruction. You love when I love your instruction and I want to be fully alive as the one you created me to be. I acknowledge right now that I am at my best when I trust and obey you, God. I find delight in knowing and seeing that the earth is filled with your love. I see it all around me and as I know you more, I only come to know your more of your love.

THANKS
BE TO
GOD

TWENTY-NINE

THANKS BE TO GOD FOR GRATITUDE AND PEACE

"Let the peace of Christ rule in your hearts, since as members of one body you were called to peace. And be thankful. Let the message of Christ dwell among you richly as you teach and admonish one another with all wisdom through psalms, hymns, and songs from the Spirit, singing to God with gratitude in your hearts. And whatever you do, whether in word or deed, do it all in the name of the Lord Jesus, giving thanks to God the Father through him."

PSALMS 119:57-64 NIV

Thanks be to God for peace that rules in my heart and for thankfulness that I can choose to walk in, in every season. Jesus, you supply the peace I need. I don't have to make it up for myself or hope I can find some lying on the side of the road. True peace is a gift that no one but you can give me. I am so thankful for the blessing of peace. I want the world around me to know this peace that surpasses all understanding. As I know you more, the knowledge of you simmers in my soul and creates an aroma of Christ as you are the fragrance rising from me. Let it simmer and dwell in me richly. I pray it would be reflected in the way I love the ones you have placed around me - in my teaching, singing and gratitude from my heart to the heart of God. I pray no matter who hears the words from my mouth there would be one name they remember - Jesus. Let all that I do be done in the name of the Lord Jesus Christ.

THANKS
BE TO
GOD

THIRTY

THANKS BE TO GOD FOR GRATITUDE AND PEACE

"After taking the cup, he gave thanks and said, "Take this and divide it among you. For I tell you I will not drink again from the fruit of the vine until the kingdom of God comes." And he took bread, gave thanks and broke it, and gave it to them, saying, "This is my body given for you; do this in remembrance of me.""

LUKE 22:17-19 NIV

Thanks be to God our Father, for Jesus Christ our Lord, and the Holy Spirit our advocate. Jesus, there is no one like you. The holy son of God who put on flesh to dwell with us, our teacher and servant king, our example, the suffering servant who defeated death and the grave. You rose again in victory and you are coming back again. How could I comprehend that my own debt has been paid in full. My king, my savior and friend. You have made me right and I could have never been right in my own strength. I will remember your body broken and blood poured out that gave me life. Thanks be to God for this miracle of miracles - a prisoner set free, a prodigal reconciled, a broken heart redeemed. Thanks be to God for Jesus, my Savior.

THANKS
BE TO
GOD

THANKS BE

TO GOD

Thank you, friend, for coming on this journey. I have learned that I cannot count the ways I could continue to thank God. As soon as I think I have seen His goodness in my life, He has already been good again and left me with yet another reason to praise. Whether seeing Him in the middle of the darkest night or walking with Him on the mountain peaks, I have seen and I will see His goodness in the land of the living (Psalm 27:13 NIV). My prayer for you is that as you close these 30 days, they are a voice that will carry into your future thanks and praise to God. As you step forward into a new season, it is my hope that you would walk with the phrase near to the door of your mouth, "Thanks be to God."

www.ingramcontent.com/pod-product-compliance
Lightning Source LLC
Chambersburg PA
CBHW040133150726
48005CB00015B/2480